DISNEY
THE
LION KING

IDEA
LAB

Shaina Olmanson

Lerner Publications ◆ Minneapolis

For Anna Jacobson and all the
students at Falcon Heights Elementary

The photographs in this book were created by Shaina Olmanson.
Special thanks to hand models Miles Stuart, Oliver Tran, Kjell Olmanson, and
Magnus Olmanson.

Lerner Publications Company
A division of Lerner Publishing Group, Inc.
241 First Avenue North
Minneapolis, MN 55401 USA

For reading levels and more information, look up this title at www.lernerbooks.com.

Main body text set in Mikado a 14/18.
Typeface provided by HVD Fonts.

Library of Congress Cataloging-in-Publication Data

Names: Olmanson, Shaina, author.
Title: The Lion King idea lab / by Shaina Olmanson.
Description: Minneapolis, MN : Lerner Publishing Group, Inc., [2020] | Series: Disney
    STEAM projects | Includes bibliographical references and index. | Audience: Ages
    7–11. | Audience: Grades K to 3.
Identifiers: LCCN 2018054257 (print) | LCCN 2018055350
    (ebook) | ISBN 9781541561595 (eb pdf) | ISBN 9781541554856 (lb : alk. paper) |
    ISBN 9781541574045 (pb : alk. paper)
Subjects: LCSH: Handicraft—Juvenile literature. | Science—Experiments—Juvenile
    literature. | Lion King (Motion picture)—Juvenile literature. | Africa—Social life and
    customs—Juvenile literature.
Classification: LCC TT160 (ebook) | LCC TT160 .O46 2020 (print) | DDC 745.5—dc23

LC record available at https://lccn.loc.gov/2018054257

Manufactured in the United States of America
1-45803-42685-3/29/2019

Contents

The World of *The Lion King*

Simba and Nala wanted to learn about the Pride Lands outside of their home at Pride Rock. Together, they set off to explore.

Do you wonder about the world around you? Are you interested in how nature works? Explore the Pride Lands—and beyond—through science, technology, engineering, art, and math right in your own home!

Before You Get Started

Safety is important as you create. A clean workspace helps to keep you safe. Cover it with newspaper or cardboard. This makes it easy to clean up too!

Gather the materials you need before you start each project. Most of the projects in this book use supplies you can find around your home, online, or at a craft or hardware store. Some projects require you to use sharp objects or hot tools. Ask an adult for permission to use the tools and materials before you start.

Zazu Fliers

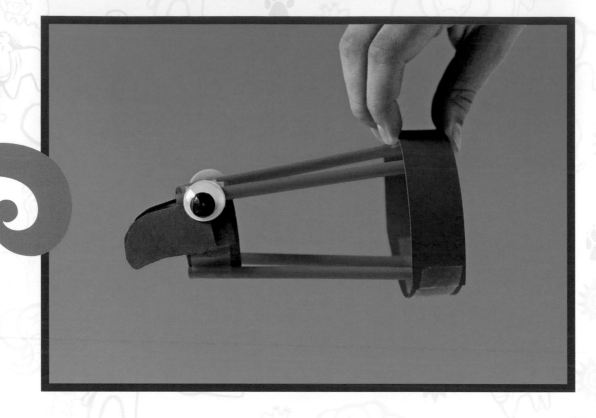

Make your own hornbill-inspired plane with straws and paper, and send the Zazu flier soaring.

Materials

- scissors
- ruler
- blue cardstock
- clear tape
- four plastic straws
- orange cardstock
- googly eyes

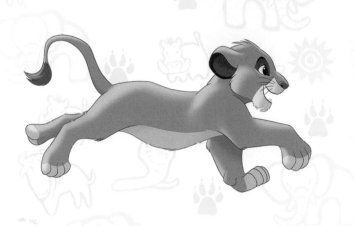

1. Cut two 1-inch (2.5 cm) strips from the blue cardstock along the long edge of the paper. Cut one strip in half.

2. Tape the long strip and one of the shorter strips to create two loops.

3. Cut the straws to 5 inches (13 cm) long. Make sure to cut off any bendy parts of the straws.

4. Tape one end of each straw to the inside of the larger loop, evenly spacing them around the circle.

5. Keeping the straws evenly spaced, tape the other end of each straw to the outside of the smaller loop.

6. Make a beak for your flier out of the orange cardstock. Tape it to the smaller loop. Tape googly eyes to either side of your flier.

7. Your Zazu flier is ready to soar! Try changing the length of the straws or the size of the loops to see how it affects your plane's flight.

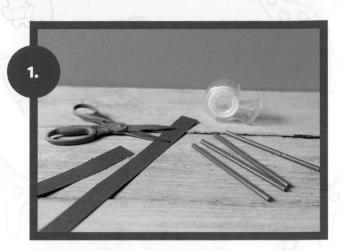

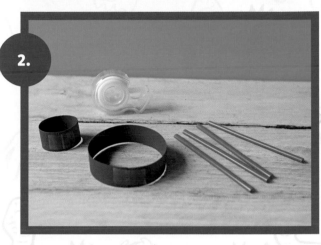

Simba Mosaic

Rafiki marks Simba's birth by drawing him on a tree. Design a piece of mosaic art like Rafiki's drawing of Simba.

Materials
- clear CD case
- marker
- lentils and beans of different colors
- white glue
- tweezers (optional)

1. Open the CD case. Draw an outline of Simba's shape on one inner side of the CD case.

2. Sort the beans and lentils by shape and color. Think about creating a pattern with the lentils and beans within the Simba outline. You can also fill the area outside the outline using different colors.

3. Cover an area of the CD case with glue. Place beans and lentils on the glue. You can use tweezers to help place them.

4. Continue gluing beans and lentils to the CD case until it is covered. Let the glue dry completely. Close the CD case and display your artwork.

STEAM Takeaway

A mosaic is a decoration made of small pieces of glass, stone, or other items. Artists arrange the pieces in a design to create a work of art.

Pride Rock Model

Pride Rock is home to Simba and the lion pride. You can build a model of Pride Rock using craft sticks.

Materials
- bamboo skewers or toothpicks
- scissors
- craft sticks of different sizes
- small items, such as coins or paper clips

4a.

1. If using bamboo skewers, get an adult's help to cut off the sharp ends. Then cut the skewers in half.

2. Using the craft sticks and bamboo skewers or toothpicks, create a bridge and towers to look like Pride Rock. Start at the base and work your way up.

3. Try different ways to create the pieces of Pride Rock. One way is to layer the sticks together.

4. Lay one stick on a flat surface. Place two sticks about 1 inch (2.5 cm) apart the opposite way, on top of the first stick so the ends overlap. Place another stick parallel to the first stick, halfway down the overlapping sticks.

4b.

5. While holding the top stick flat, weave two more sticks into the center, under the bottommost stick and over the topmost stick.

6. Add a stick underneath the last two sticks. Weave sticks on either side. Continue adding sticks and watch as the bridge forms. Add additional structures to your bridge to complete the model.

7. When your model is finished, test it by placing small items on the bridge to see if it can hold them. If it collapses, think of ways you can make your Pride Rock stronger, such as building a larger base or using a different combination of sticks. Then try again.

STEAM Takeaway

Engineering uses science to make new things. An engineer creates a design for a new object and thinks about the best materials to use. If a design doesn't work, engineers try new designs and materials. You just used engineering to create a model of Pride Rock!

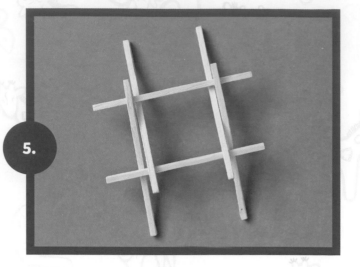

5.

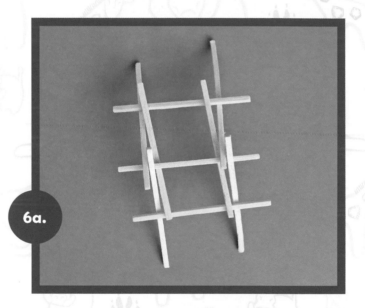

6a.

6b.

Look at the Stars Telescope

Mufasa tells Simba that the stars are always there to guide him through life. Get a better view of the stars by making a telescope.

Materials
- markers, paints, or crayons
- 2 paper towel tubes
- scissors
- lenses from a pair of reading glasses
- masking tape

1. Decorate the outside of the paper towel tubes.

1.

2. Cut one of the paper towel tubes lengthwise. Roll the tube so the cut sides overlap and the tube is smaller in width than the uncut tube. Place one end of the rolled tube inside the uncut paper towel tube. Adjust how tightly the inside tube is rolled until it slides in and out smoothly.

3. You can find reading glasses at the dollar store, or ask an adult for permission before using an old pair of glasses. Have an adult help you push out the lenses.

2a.

STEAM Takeaway

The lenses help more light reach your eye. They bend the light, making what you see appear larger. Different lens curves can change the size of the image you see. Changing the reading glasses lenses can change how your telescope works.

2b.

4. Tape one lens to the end of the inside tube. The lens should curve to face inside the tube.

5. Tape the second lens to the outside tube at the other end of the telescope. This lens should curve to face away from the tube.

6. To view the stars or something far away, look through the lens of the inside tube. Find something in the distance, and use your telescope to make it appear closer. To focus your telescope, slide the outside tube in or out.

4.

5.

Melting Moon Bridge Art

Timon and Pumbaa help Simba learn to live life with fewer worries. Use old crayon bits and heat to create carefree, moonlit artwork of the three friends.

Materials
- old crayons
- small white poster board
- pencil
- blue painter's tape
- white glue
- hair dryer
- black permanent marker

1. Remove paper wrappers from the crayons. Break crayons into small pieces.

2. On the poster board, draw the outline shapes of Simba, Pumbaa, and Timon walking across the log bridge in front of the full moon.

3. Cover the moon with painter's tape.

4. Glue pieces of crayon in a line across the top of the poster board. Let the glue dry completely.

5. Prop the poster board up so it is standing upright. Put newspaper or another covering under it because the crayons drip off the board as they melt. With help from an adult, blow hot air from the hair dryer over the crayons until they melt and start to run.

6. Angle the hair dryer so the crayons drip down the white areas of the poster board. Continue until most of the poster board is covered with melted crayon. While the melted crayon is still warm, remove the painter's tape. Let the poster board cool.

7. Use the black marker to color in Simba, Pumbaa, Timon, and the log.

Circuit Bugs

When Simba joins Timon and Pumbaa, he learns the slimy yet satisfying joy of eating bugs. Create your own creepy-crawly bug that actually moves.

Materials

- scissors
- toothbrush
- double-sided foam tape
- small vibrating motor
- coin cell battery
- pipe cleaner
- googly eyes

1.

1. Have an adult help you cut off the handle of the toothbrush.

2. Cut a piece of foam tape to fit the toothbrush head. Stick one side of the tape to the back of the toothbrush head.

3. Attach the motor to the other side of the foam tape, leaving room on one side of the tape for the battery.

4. Place one wire from the motor on the foam tape. Place the battery on top of the wire, pressing it down hard to secure it to the tape.

4.

5. Cut another small piece of tape. Attach it to the end of the other wire.

6. Tie a pipe cleaner around the center of the toothbrush head, and cut it to act as antennas. Attach googly eyes to the front of your bug.

6a.

6b.

7. When you are ready to see your circuit bug move, place the exposed end of the wire between the pipe cleaners and the battery. Hold the wire in place with the foam tape you placed on the end. The wire must touch the battery to turn the bug on.

STEAM Takeaway

Your bug uses a motor and a battery to move. When you connect the motor to the battery, you create an electrical circuit. This makes the motor run, which causes the toothbrush head to vibrate and move.

Rain in a Jar

During the drought, food is hard to find near Pride Rock. Rain is necessary for animals to drink and plants to grow. Create your own rainstorm in a jar.

Materials
- large clear jar
- water
- blue food dye
- small dish
- shaving cream foam
- plastic dropper

1. Fill the jar with water, about 1 inch (2.5 cm) from the top.

2. Mix together 5 drops of blue food dye and 2 tablespoons of water in a small dish.

3. Spray shaving cream foam to fill the jar opening.

4. Using the dropper, carefully drop the blue water onto the shaving cream. Watch as the blue "rain" fills the "cloud" and then enters the jar.

STEAM Takeaway

Water vapor in the sky sticks together to form clouds. When drops of water in the clouds get heavy enough, gravity pulls the drops down as rain. The falling drops are denser than the clouds. In your jar, gravity pulls the blue "raindrops" down through the shaving cream "cloud."

Lioness String Art

Nala and the lionesses help Simba fight Scar at Pride Rock. You can make a roaring lioness for your wall.

Materials
- pencil
- square wood block
- small finishing nails
- hammer
- scissors
- string or embroidery floss in several colors

1. Draw an outline of Nala or your favorite lioness on the wood block.

2. With an adult's help, place nails ½ inch (1.3 cm) apart along the outline and use the hammer to pound them into the wood. Leave at least ½ inch of each nail sticking out from the wood block.

3. Cut a long piece of string or embroidery floss. Tie the string to one nail.

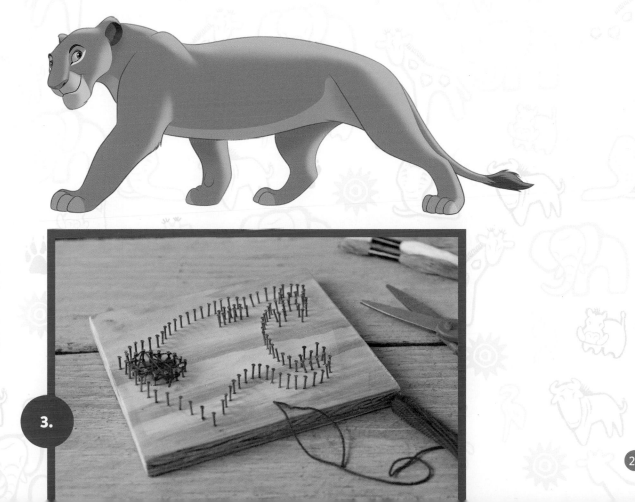

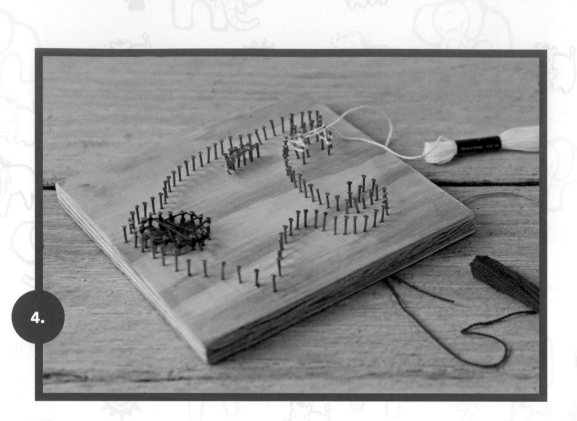

4. Weave the string between the nails to create a pattern. Pull the string tight when you wrap it around the next nail. Tie the string off when you are done with the color and cut off any excess.

5. Continue weaving string of different colors until you have the design you want. Try creating shapes and patterns with the string!

Glossary

circuit: the complete path of an electric current

drought: a period with little or no rain

focus: adjust to give a clear view

gravity: a force that draws objects together

parallel: lying in the same direction without meeting

pattern: a repeated design

vapor: a substance in the form of a gas

vibrate: to move back and forth or from side to side very quickly

width: how wide something is, or the distance from one side of an object to the other side of the object

To Learn More

Books

Ahrens, Niki. *Aladdin Idea Lab*. Minneapolis: Lerner Publications, 2020.
Explore the world of *Aladdin* through science, technology, engineering, art, and math projects.

Mould, Steve. *How to Be a Scientist*. New York: DK, 2017.
Learn how to think like a scientist by following along with step-by-step experiments.

Websites

10 Lion Facts!
https://www.natgeokids.com/au/discover/animals/general-animals/10-lion-facts/
Discover amazing information about lions, such as how they hunt and how fast they can run.

Which Character from *The Lion King* Are You?
https://ohmy.disney.com/quiz/2015/10/01/quiz-which-character-from-the-lion-king-are-you/
Take a quiz to see which character from *The Lion King* you are most like.

Index

Photo Acknowledgments

Additional image credits: E_K/Shutterstock.com (gears); Belozersky/Shutterstock.com (flask); Aksenova Natalya/Shutterstock.com, p. 6 (glue); Olga Kovalenko/Shutterstock.com, p. 6 (scissors); Richard Sharrocks/Getty Images, p. 7 (crayons); SJ Travel Photo and Video/Shutterstock.com, p. 7 (paints).